the night of the lunar eclipse

Margaret Szumowski

the night of the lunar eclipse

TUPELO PRESS

The Night of the Lunar Eclipse
Copyright © 2005 Margaret Szumowski

ISBN 10: 1-932195-23-8
ISBN 13: 978-1-932195-23-1
Printed in Canada
All rights reserved.
No part of this book may be reproduced
without the permission of the publisher.

First paperback edition
Library of Congress Control Number: 2005903084

Tupelo Press
Post Office Box 539, Dorset, Vermont 05251
(802) 366-8185
(802) 362-1883 fax
editor@tupelopress.org
www.tupelopress.org

Cover and book design by Josef Beery
Cover photo of night blooming cereus by Robert G. Fovell, © 2005

contents

i. the temple of love

La Bruja   2
Iowa Springtime with Black Swans   3
By the Light of Her Flaming Baton   4
Beggars' Opera   5
At the End of Their Driveway   7
Braiding Our Hair   8
Falling Into the Tub of Divinity   9
My Mother Bathing Me   11
Translation by Water   12

ii. the space between us

The Space Between Us   14
Huge in His Red Robe   19
Tough Customer   20
Italian Moment Interrupted   22
Sky Gazer   24
La Fiorentina   25
The Madonna with Red Hair   27
I Ask for Bridge Repair   29
Asking for the Bread   30
His Fingertips   32

iii. cheating the underworld

A Woman is Trapped in a Tree   34
Welcome to Frackville   35
Falling in at Summer School   37
Falling Flat Again   38
The Roses on the Table   40
Self-Portrait in a Helicopter   41
She is a Nation   42
Where Have You Been?   43
Girl Turned to Stone   44
Salty   45
Beauty Pageant in Sarajevo   46
Him   47
Return on Fireworks Night   49

iv. we cannot extinguish the night

Driving Toward Key West   52
How Dare the Weatherman   54
Sauerkraut Supper   55
My Father Blesses the Fleet   56
We Cannot Extinguish the Night   57
Bathsheba: I Do Not Want to Love You   58
The Lover   59
Brazen   60
The Moths   62
Floating Back   63
Where Love is Stored   65
Men in Love with Les Parisiennes   66
Taking His Name in Translation   68

The Women Appear as Aurora Borealis 69
The Room Loves Her 71
Smart Bomb 72
LA in the Green Spring 73
Anatomy Class 75
Finally the Amaryllis Blooms in Late February 77
Silhouette of a Music Stand in an Empty Room 78
The Fence 79

V. the unlikely landscape of forgiveness

The Unlikely Landscape of Forgiveness 82
No Darkness Anywere 83
Forget the Kiss 84
The Knife 85
Rembrandt's House 86
Sea Wind 87
Christ Goes Out in the World 89
Night Woman's Triolet 90
The Old Man in the Midst of Renoir's Women 91
Bringing the Moon to Her for a Closer Look 92
Eve's List of What Keeps Her from Despair 94
Columbus Avenue on the Night of the Eclipse 96
Bare-Handed 97
How Far I Would Go for You 99

Acknowledgments 102

i.
the temple of love

Tell all the truth, but tell it slant.

la bruja: a ghazal

Sadly, I walk to the sea, carry bunches of roses.
La Bruja, where are you, my witch, with your bunches of roses.

Your girl wanders at midnight, black car spinning fast.
Everywhere along the sea, pockets of roses.

Your mother knew nothing but childbirth and whiskey.
Who can love this broken tree touched by roses?

Your father tends his garden, aqua vitae, magnolia, apple tree.
La bruja makes the shivering boy a lunch of roses.

A country we loved, broken and dying, now bags of dry leaves.
A man knows how to fly, how to flee, crouched in roses.

She loves wearing dresses made of spiders and cobwebs.
He tastes women's painted lips like brunches of roses.

Bare fists or knives, your father loves a good beating.
Who first kissed our garden door, its scent of roses?

Your old woman prays and dances. She stops the wild fires!
All I have is dried fruit and a crutch of roses.

Your healer lays black roses in a silver bowl.
How those pesky deer love the munch of roses.

Brett covered his scrawny body with a green tattoo.
Who was the old woman, crying, hunched in roses?

I could barely remember Margaret, my name at dawn.
In white gowns all young girls to the river. Stench of roses.

iowa springtime with black swans

Everywhere is muddy and rich—
crops sprout up green, barns burst with piglets,
calves and lambs, all good to the touch,

calves licking us with their blue tongues.
Luxuriant surprise in my homeland,
like the way we have all changed.

I love the look of black swans crossing small ponds,
preening themselves with orange beaks.
This is the Iowa I want, my father soft

with the children. He brushes the dog's coat
to gold, holds a child on each knee.
We name what is strong, wear the past

like a cloak, tendrils rise around us,
their beauty sharp against
the fresh-turned earth.

by the light of her flaming baton

She dips it in kerosene, throws it lit into the night.
She's forgotten sweep, flying eagle,

figure eight: her thumbs barely move fast enough
to keep propeller's flame spinning

red flowers in the Iowa sky.
She's forgotten how to twirl with fire

wearing a black tutu and white marching boots,
but she wants God to let her baton

fly up into the sky, see her brother bright,
constellation MICHAEL, plays his grand piano,

sails through the sky—one big opera boat—
diva's arias just for him,

and Puccini better not tremble.
His sister, the constant majorette,

sends up flares
and fireworks from far below,

flatfooted, earthbound again,
as she watches him

parasail over Lake George.
Come back, Maestro, she calls.

beggars' opera

We swung those legs from the hip,
stood up tall,
books on our heads
and books in our hands—
bookish beauties
dolled up
like some man's may basket.
Five beautiful Carson girls,
hostesses at the Gold Buffet,
majorettes in white boots,
blue-sequined tappers,
mesh tights on long legs.

Even Michael got into the act as Miss Greenfield
the day we all dressed up as Iowa towns,
Bevington, Mason City, Oskaloosa, Winterset.
Maybe he could get some attention,
dressed up for love, fat musician
plays his brilliant trombone.
"Take me, Kiss me, Gobble me up."
Michael, beggar for kisses,
and so were we, each of us looking
for a man to love
with heart and feet and teeth and hands
and hips and palms.

When Michael was ill, could barely walk,
his lover, Jesse Medina, leaned over him,
not like a fussy aunt,
not like a terrified friend,
just like a love-starved husband,
Jesse kissed the beggar with a moist loud smack.

Michael, the Beggar King,
conductor of the Beggars' Opera, kisses aplenty.
"I have known true love," he said,
and played the piano until he was too weak
to kiss the keys.

at the end of their driveway

When Father held a scalpel up

to sister's throat, Brother said,

"If you don't put down your scalpel,

Dr. Dad, I will kill you." Not

much of a surprise that scalpel

went down on the floor and Big Daddy

with it. Alive. Alive he is

by the grace of his son, but graceless

he is, as I knew on my wedding day,

sitting at the end of our driveway waiting

for him to take me to the church.

braiding our hair

I was sixteen when Mother saw God.
Her seventh pregnancy. She bled.

Every morning, she braided all six heads.
Nothing stopped her, not even bleeding.

Rita wriggled, and Cindy cried.
Mom kept twisting our hair into braids,

Mom bleeding, Susan whining. She kept braiding,
put all of us on the bus and drove to the hospital.

They couldn't find her veins. He said
she would die. *You have to help me.*

I need you, he said. I dressed the little
girls, braided their hair. He looked

at me and reached. *Mom, Mom*, I cried.
Then Mother saw God. She told Him

she had to live for her children. She had to
save us from him. Lost baby.

Every day she kept braiding our hair.
More babies and sex with him

every night
on the loud bed.

falling into the tub of divinity

I stand over the stove for hours,
watch temperature's tedious rise to hard boil,
my hands burning from steam rising off

yellow bubbling mass, then marshmallow cream,
chocolate chips and walnuts,
sticky rich candy.

Sometimes we children taste candy,
foil-wrapped packages stored
in the frozen cellar. Hungry for sweetness,

we stuff ourselves,
so much candy it could be a factory,
fudge, pralines, best of all white frothy candy.

Can you cook it up like the divinity of our youth?
Can you taste and see and find it delicious?
Can you stand over a hot stove

waiting with your hand burning
from stirring that swirling mass,
hot enough to kill anyone

who falls in the tub of divinity.
Let us remember despite everything
divinity is cooked up in this house

sweet and only at Christmas,
light and abundant enough to be shared with neighbors.
Old Mrs. McNamara with her mean cat Bismark

that bit little Peggy in the cheek
receives divinity. Blue-green spruces
reach all the way to heaven.

The Callisons get some too
even if Butch packed
little Peggy's nose with mud.

At Christmas, fudge and divinity
for all, Monsignor Higgins bearing Waterford Crystal—
unbroken never-used crystal—the broken

Cunninghams and their wild brood,
and the father chokes on divinity,
tasting and seeing and finding it delicious as hell.

my mother bathing me

I am thirty years old and my mother sponges
my big pregnant belly, washes me carefully
with warm water and a washcloth—

up as far as possible, down as far as possible,
and then wash possible. She laughs, scared
of losing me. Mother's come to bathe me

and stay with me and help me hold on
to this wild baby dancing up a storm
on the dangerous placenta. Michael visits

in dreams. *I'm all right, Mother,* he says,
I'm playing in the upstairs orchestra. Losing me
seems possible. She feeds me small bits

of chicken salad and washes me. We play
three games of Scrabble every day. Fiercely good
at Scrabble, I spell out huge words with every letter

I have, *ecstasy, releve, surging, crescendo.* She laughs,
struggles, moves her letters around. I lie dreaming
in my bed, loving as she did, the rolling world

in my belly. I remember the black velvet off-the-shoulder
gown I never saw her wear, thick red lipstick, golden glittering
dresses and spike heels on New Year's Eve, my mother

at the machine trailing ruffles, tangled in red, new net
around the bassinet, bathing infants, rocking and suckling
them in the nursery, rhymes at midnight. Father calls,
Come home, Georgia.

translation by water

I am translated, moon-bellied,
a creature of tides.

Floating this meadowed sea,
I finger the reeds.

Orange fins hatching, blizzards
of white butterflies.

The sea breathes. I float
faceless in water

sharp with teeth. A tide
could break me against the shore.

The razor-toothed,
the shovel-faced scooping

the slime. This is moon time.
The coursing of tides,
        the innermost sea.

ii.
the space between us

The edge of good, the tongue of evil.

the space between us

Blood everywhere even if we can't see it. 2000 gladiators dead,
    hundreds of elk, zebra, tigers, wild horses, hippopotami.

Empty now except for the tourists. A woman poses in front of the coliseum
    as if it were a football stadium complete with marching band.

The woman, just a tourist, the coliseum broken, ribs showing.
    In the catacombs, the partially-severed head of Cecelia. That good woman.

I wear a loose blue sweater and behind me
    the fields ripple with poppies. The world

looks new in the Italian spring, and I am younger than ever.
    Andrew says people think I'm his daughter. No danger of that.

Just call me a youthful Athena struggling
    to make sense of it all, weeping over thousands of ancient bodies.

In his red martyr robe, the priest says Mass in the cave. The early popes
    step out to greet us. The good ones, enslaved, beheaded, crucified—

wander the catacombs looking for Christ. Everywhere a balancing
    on the edge of good, on the tongue of evil.

Duomos and shrines and visits to 1600 year old saints.
    They occupy Italy and no one forgets them. They speak up for themselves.

At the Vatican, I carry my journal. I note all assumptions,
    resurrections and transfigurations. We jump from cobblestone

to cobblestone, lit up for each other and Italy. See how light
    pours on us. At the Vatican, I wear a purple velvet jacket.
        "Call me, Monsignor!"

She looks to be in her 20's, me, that silly traveler. She's chugging up
    and down the Grand Canal on the crowded vaporetto,

a merry bunch of children laughing. Already they know
    hands are part of the message. Andrew, at ease, sips his wine.

He makes love to her twice every day in Venice.
    They decide to stay in Italy forever.

We never escape, thousands of Poles dead
    at Monte Cassino, monastery destroyed four times.

Mother drove German prisoners over a mined road.
    All around, green mountains, the winding switchbacks

of narrow road. Then, the Polish cemetery. Irena and Jan alive.
    Roses and lilies in the monastery garden.

Andrew leans against marble in the Vatican. An angel with wings
    the length of her body, her female bottom much patted.

On the vaporetto, a finger runs across my rear. Everyone looks
    almost innocent.

We run wild in Italy, through the green hills, past the catacombs
    and broken aqueduct, linger by the Trevi Fountain,

watch the stone horses, their perpetual fight with Neptune,
    that greedy god who would keep them in his kingdom.

The horses leap out of the Trevi, too big to be trapped in the pool
    with Neptune. He's got a grip on them and a grip on us.

I'm ready to ride away on my Vespa, that new trick I've picked up
    from the Italian women in high heels & fancy dresses,

fishnet stockings. The canal, murky and beautiful. Buildings
   sinking, their delicate yellows and pinks. Some remnants

of gilt. Someone's gondola parked next to his home on the water.
   I hop in and hope for a kiss. Ah, la dolce vita.

At the coliseum, crowds crawl over the pitted ruin. They are ready
   to martyr the Christians.

Even the lions are sick of death. They growl like peace-lovers about
   arrows stuck in Sebastian, Lucia's lost eyes.

Her dried up bony feet scared me—Lucia wrapped in one
   of Italy's bright poppies. Dangerous and beautiful and dead.

Even the tigers are tender towards the martyred.
   The angel whispers to Abraham, "Do not kill Isaac!"

Thank you, dear angel! The dead lie down, comforted
   in their underground world.

Here I am in my blue sweater again, a color my mother never liked.
   I wear the sweater every day.

Poppies and grass. I lie down in this field
   next to the buried. So what if I'm alive and they're dead?

The pines and cypresses and I are alive. On my way to Quo Vadis
   Domine, hoping for peace, my breasts seem fuller,
      or did I forget to notice them,

so busy with children. What use are they? These protuberances,
   these cabbage roses beloved by men, these pets of theirs.
      All the madonnas with breasts unlikely.

They extend from their clavicles. Or at a right angle that couldn't
help but hurt. Oh, the breasts in Italy, the beautiful small,
large, strange breasts. Lost breasts.

I lean against a frail fence at the coliseum waiting to be executed—
and all for the beauty of these breasts. Thought you were
smarter than this, didn't you?

Andrew's familiar endearing posture in front of San Marco,
his head slightly tilted. He stands mostly on his left foot,

and behind him, the plaza where we danced the waltz all night,
then walked over so many bridges, lost on the wrong canal.

Bruno, come back to us. We won't do to you what they did.
Beneath your statue in Campo dei Fiori, the inevitable
accordian player

hopes for a little money in his hat. Bruno in his monk's robe,
steps down to point out the sun and planets. The flat and
treacherous earth he fell from.

And me, smiling at some fellow on the bridge. Could it be
Andrew taking me on some wild ride again. She looks happy,
almost too much light!

What is she doing, sitting by the Arno, the Ponte Vecchio in the
background? Men rowing for centuries.

Maybe it's not her fault, wind blowing her scarf, jacket slipping off
her shoulder, her breasts taking up too much space in the picture

when the Ponte Vecchio deserves all the attention? If I stay in Italy
much longer, I'll be riding a Vespa. You saw the picture. Me in a
velvet jacket

and black tights ready to mount the Vespa and take off into
the Italian night. Andrew says I'm learning how to live.

If I had power, if I were Wisdom, I'd say that evil does not have
the face of a woman, the way Michelangelo, and all the church
fathers painted us.

Every day in Italy, we listen to terror in the Middle East,
suicide bombings, and we, walking the Apian Way, looking
at saints in every church,

cannot transform the world outside, no matter how beautiful
the transfiguration, no matter how many strong men lift
Christ from the cross,

how many gorgeous madonnas pick up the holy one, who holds
Mary's thumb with one hand and blesses us with the other.

Michelangelo was right
when he left that space between us.

huge in his red robe

God is huge in his red robe letting go with a battering of wings,
geese, herons, swans, seagulls, hawks, condors, halibut, haddock,
pickerel, barracuda, basking whale, right whale, great whale,

porpoises and seals,

thundering toward the sea, and he, bigger than all of them, pushing
them to life, sending them gustily over the high sea and behind him
a dog, a cat, some shadowy mammals,

no humans so far,

to be driven into the sea, driven out of paradise, out of war-
torn countries, driven to drink, to kill, to love,
to dance the tarantella or the dance of death, to play the tuba,

to play the trumpet, swing from the trapeze,

compose music, to be Mozart, to be the darkness of Wagner,
to build the pyramids, to divide themselves into warring tribes, to blast
one another, to paint the hand of God almost touching us, to yell at God,

to hate God for what happened,

to go to God despite what happened, to pray or not to pray, to prey upon
one another, to keep God, or to let go of him with whatever consequences.
A vigorous God, an excited God. One that allows us

to love God for what happened—

all the energy of animal creation
bursting upon the earth, the earth reeling with hooves, fish splashing,
the tidal wave of creation bursting upon the earth,

and then he touches us.

tough customer

       I could float in a lagoon of badness,
draw men into my gondola,
but only a dope

chooses John the Baptist
as her first customer.

       Fresh from living on swamp grass
and mosquito wings, he turns
those eyes on me.

Would you get into my boat,
spread the canopy of trees for cover,
wear soft air for clothes? I offer.

       He looks at me with eyes
that nail my soul to the twisted bayou tree,
must be related to Nathan,

the buzzard who tormented David.
His glare crumbles my bones.

       I'll have to go back to the city
and get to work, but not
the kind of work I had in mind.

My soul a flaming petal.
Roots straight to hell. The real me
evil as licorice. I'm the devil's cancan girl.

The prophet laughs,
Woman soft as magnolia,
you fall, petals onto the earth.

You better ride the sloop Desire
straight to paradise
to the lover you long for.

italian moment interrupted

Your lips delicious. Venice nothing like
love in Des Moines, Iowa

where we swam, dined at Babe's
and rolled in the museum's

rose-filled gardens.
As a young girl I saw a naked statue

in that very museum. A boy naked
showing his penis!

We girls turned our heads,
then looked back quick to see.

On our honeymoon,
Dad called to see what we were doing.

He sneaked into our night.
But let's get back to San Marco,

and forget about him.
I'll erase him from the poem soon.

We are such lovers in Venice,
on and off the vaporetto,

and the bridge of sighs.
You love the beautiful carnival masks.

Later we learn that men wearing those masks
sneak into convents.

A scary side to the story like our story
of Dad sneaking into our bedroom.

In Venice, we give no thought to him.
We are in the presence of everyday Italians.

We pretend to be Italian.
No one sneaks into our room.

sky gazer

He is walking in the garden,
and he looks into her face.

She can't manage all that ecstatic
looking at God

without being propped up.
Everything is dangerous:

the cats and grackles,
the weight of her own gorgeous flowers.

In the garden
the sky gazer lilies shiver,

their brilliant stamens,
burnt orange,

and the center of each lily,
sticky as honey.

la fiorentina

This food is too rich for us,
pastas, scaloppini, rigatoni, parmesan,
deep purple wine. We order only espresso
dark and bitter, none of your pink
Italian cookies. Let us drink black,
and chew crusts until we're thin and strong
as old sailors who know only the taste
of salt. But even old Batista

the pizza man, looks different here.
He wears his rags like a velvet cloak
looks at us like some grand signor
examining his jewels. The coffee machine
is a golden palace, walls of emerald
and silver, every cake plump with custard,
air heavy as honey,

and ah, the foaming milk, the thick icing.
Old men savor last night's loves,
rich cakes gobbled too quickly. I hear
the women chant, "Almond, almond,
they taste of almond every one."
Put on your velvet doublet, your tights.
Trim your beard to a goatee, remember wild nights

on the riverbank, water swelling
around us, dark rivers of our bodies.
We are not spectators in a museum,
only watching the Renaissance creatures,
we are great golden bodies
heavy as cake, as bread, as all things
good to eat. I am still hungry,
let me taste you again.

the madonna with red hair

From the look on the face of the Madonna
with red hair, I know she couldn't bear
exorcisms, or Lucia's dried up feet

from the 4th century, or the plague,
and how it killed almost everyone.
No wonder they needed a piece of the true cross,

even if it wasn't.
Perhaps I underestimate this young woman
and her red-haired baby. Hair the color Christ

never saw in Palestine. She is lovely,
her baby perfect except for his trick of holding up
his fingers like a god or bishop. She's so young

and delicate. I know
what she doesn't. It's lurking
in every bone of her body. Call me if you need me,

I say with sorrow.
Michelangelo is about to play Nicodemus.
He wants to take care of these beloved friends.

He is very tired
from the ache in his back. I'm not sorry
for you, Michelangelo. You gave the snake

a woman's face. I must be Nicodemus
this time, holding Jesus, Mary, the Magdalen.
I'll hold the whole church together

with my own weak body
since God doesn't know what to do,
and everything is cracking.

i ask for bridge repair

Maybe it's only been a rope bridge after all,
the kind that swings back and forth across a chasm.

A chasm between us, and I broke the bridge.
I'm not dead but nearly so, lying

at the bottom of the gorge, not strong
enough to climb the rock and weave the strands

I myself have broken. I hurt you. I scared you.
It was a beauty of a bridge. Crossed

wild territory, huge pine trees, aspen leaves
that quivered silver in the wind.

I saw a young deer leap across the divide
where cliffs come close.

Without this bridge, I can't get to the other side.
I don't think you want to help. You want

me broken. You want this broken bridge
and me to hang here swinging against the cliff.

I deserve abandonment, having wanted the forest
the bridge and you, whom I had

no business wanting,
but wanting was its own bridge.

asking for the bread

The crowd wants him passing out fishes
and dancing in the Piazza San Marco.
I wish I'd been brave enough to ask him to waltz,

but then Andrew is a sweet waltzer,
and who knows if Jesus can dance.
He invited us to the last supper, but I was so shy,

I sat on the floor at his feet.
I didn't have the courage to stand up and reach
for the bread. This Christ so vigorous

no one could refuse him. Except one.
Me, the scared woman on the floor.
Surely, I did not refuse the bread at the last supper.

He gently pulled me up
in front of those men and gave me the bread
I was afraid to take. Who could refuse him?

Was I the one refusing this vigorous Christ?
And what was he doing in Florence?
The Doge knows nothing of this young man,

as he floats the Adriatic in his many-oared
buccarino. Everywhere Christ crucified, and
giving out bread and the Doge looking

for splendor and manly men to take the oars
of his golden vessel while people line up for bits
of the true cross. The winsomeness of Christ

is irresistible. Who wouldn't float the canals,
or even the Adriatic with him after that last supper.
I would, I tell myself,

knowing how I love the sea,
and men who can navigate
terrifying waters.

his fingertips

White heron watching. Parents, quiet—
one son finds happiness, the other in his black clothes.

Michael's fingers sure of rippling connection to the keys,
his music: shadows, aching. I give myself up to floating,

slow time, herons standing still, finally raising their wings.
Andrew and I want to be light enough

to dance at Steve's wedding, our bodies one shadow
by the bayou. The crazy trombones Steve

and Michael played, golden slides on roller coaster rides.
Steve had the good sense to marry Jenny Lee Mayfield

from Lafayette, Louisiana. Jenny in the gown her mother made,
satin and lace, flourish of pink and purple flowers in her hair.

Michael in his black clothes, pounding somber Rachmaninov.
Sweaty, we dance to zydeco, listen to Big George play washboard,

eat crawfish and crab and shrimp with spicy sauce, float
the Atchafalaya, likely to drown in the bayou, not trusting

our lives to old Pierre, trusting Michael to no one.
White heron watching. God lets us
       slip from his fingers.

iii.
cheating the underworld

"I felt my life with both hands to see if it was there."

– Emily Dickinson

a woman is trapped in a tree

I can hear her heart beating. Like a child,
she holds out her arms to be lifted up.
I know she is warm,

snow melts from her body.
I give her a bird-feeder bracelet.
All the birds build nests in her branches.

Good luck! Good luck!
You are a bird tree full of bright feathers.
You have the best view of anyone, blue hills,

forsythia bursting to bloom.
We will keep the rough boys from touching
your delicate bark.

Inside that tree her breasts are round,
her thighs are sweet, untouched.
She reaches for the evergreen, imagines

the scent of pine, the way needles brush
lips, rough petals of pine cones, the great
weight of him. She would give anything

to be a woman, to love a man,
to come out of that tree.
Bless her, oh bless her, you gods
who have no hearts.

welcome to frackville

Not McAdoo, not Promised Land,
Frackville with tedious houses and one-way streets
lined with filling stations and stone birds. Frackville,
what a place to be stuck.

The time of my maximum abundance,
and I'm stuck in drippy Frackville
next to the railroad tracks, in an all night diner
that serves nothing but macaroni and cheese.

No sexy guys in Frackville, no jazz bands, never heard
of Ma Rainey or BB King. Elvis, for certain sure, never
appeared in Frackville. No sweet guitars or Fast Eddie's
ready to dance the night away. I was disgruntled in Frackville,

kicking my shoes off, stuffing my soul with sawdust and macaroni.
Then along came Fast Eddie. The night stars moved
into Frackville, and we started up Fast Eddie's
Dance Parlor and Saloon.

What a place Eddie's was, how we trotted the floor,
how we lavished our embraces on no-good men, sipped
their dangerous lips, did the bump with their rotating hips.
Fast Eddie's where the fast guys met the faster girls,

and some—just high school girls dressed up like 25.
But everything seemed okay at Eddie's, those guys
doing the bugaloo, mashed potato, twist,
a little cha-cha, mambo, mambo.

We changed Frackville to Fast Eddyville,
and those townspeople loved it, turned out
on city streets tapping down the night,
lifting their honeys to the wild winds.

falling in at summer school

That Iowa City summer, we took the wrong courses,
met the wrong men. Patty, my roommate from Duchesne,
and I, freshly escaped from St. Catherine's, tanned ourselves

on the burning asphalt roof of Curry Hall, pretended
Paris at Joe's Bar, flirted with Frank in phony French.
After a few beers, none of those guys doubted:

we were Parisiennes, loved wine,
had lingered too many nights by the Seine.
Who registered us that summer? I was eighteen,

Transformational Linguistics, Kissing 123,
Latin American Developments,
my first C's ever. What Patty and I wanted

was Cedar River rising,
Coral Reservoir in the dark, swim the quarry,
suits slipping as we climbed the raft.

No, No, No, we said,
or I think we said, or I claim we said. Did we say no?
We went to the riverbank, let the river rise,

two shy girls from Catholic schools, and sometimes we knew
we'd never be loved like this again. One man
leaned me so far over the water to kiss me,
                                      I thought I'd fall in.

falling flat again

I promised myself I wouldn't fall flat again.
I promised I wouldn't fall for the Flat Earth
again. Hell, there are plenty of Flat Earth

types hangin' around here.
I promised I wouldn't be flat.
I promised I wouldn't stop dancing.

I promised myself a lollapalooza in June.
I promised myself that whatever George said
was probably true.

The hell with promises.
I promised I would lift myself
out of the blues. I like to sing the blues.

I like to wing the blues. I like to wing myself
out of the blues. Ain't Misbehavin,'
but I better not stay stuck in the blues.

I promised I wouldn't think of you, all night,
all day. Won't worry about you
all night, 'specially between twilight and dawn.

I promised myself not to sit by the window
all night waiting for you to come walkin'
up the street at 2AM, black car spinning away.

I promised myself you'd be swell!
I promised myself I would find out
what would make you feel swell.

I tried to get you to whirligig
your way out of this place. I promised to love
you 'til the galaxies fell out of the heavens,

and the black holes turned to light. I promise
I'll love you forever, crazy as I am for you,
crazy as you've made me, crazy with love
for you, Crazy Mama that I am.

the roses on the table

I put her on the table,
and give her a bouquet of roses.
She looks so pretty in the smell of roses.

I put my anger at her on the table.
God stirs up my soul.
He wishes my soul would breathe.

I put a juicy apple on the table.
I put my nightmare next to it.
The nightmare eats my sweet apple.

I won't wear my bravery on my shirt.
I have no bravery.
God is stirring my cowardly soul.

I don't believe he's stirring my soul.
I know I have no soul left.
I say God has gone fishing.

I say God has gone fishing for her.
I say that God has let her go.
I put all my sorrow on the table.

She goes into darkness and pretends
it is light. I am sorry for the poor African
in the pew behind me. She has the sorrows

that won't go away. She can't leave them
on the table. I can't leave her on the table.
But where will I put her so she won't break?

self-portrait in a helicopter

I can land on a slip of paper, I tell myself.
Why wasn't I able to find her that whole night?
Maybe it was the false address and phone number.

I landed the helicopter carefully on the mayor's roof,
and crept down the back stairs.
I thought it was his son Hades again, the one covered

with a green tattoo. An undercover agent, I crept
round the city, knocked at doors, looked everywhere,
avoiding the attack dogs. I even lifted

the manhole covers, searched the alleys.
Sometimes I enjoy my helicopter, its churning whirring
turning relaxes me after another day of looking for her

at Hades Barbecue, the Rave, the Lunatic's
Dance Hall, the Monster's Den. And she's nowhere.

she is a nation

She is a nation gone wrong,
every road shut down,

emaciated refugees crowding the streets
ululating for the latest death.

She shaves her head, wears black,
beats her knuckles against the bars.

Virunga cut down for firewood.
She loves frogs and salamanders,

small snakes and caterpillars.
The woman and the nation, not talking,

the country stripped of trees and singing frogs.
A nation where suddenly

those who live close together,
slice down their neighbors,

neighbors so close the killers
are cutting their very own throats.

An old man sits reading his Bible
near Lake Kivu. Children offer trays of peanuts

for change, and men sell fetishes.
She suffers, a slashed nation,

windows painted black, eyes shut,
lips sewn silent. At the mission

a woman throws herself
to the crocodiles.

where have you been?

I've been to Marlboro to pick up Martha, worried about her girl.
    We go together to the place of worry.
I've been to the House of Worry. I have been to the House of Terror.
I've gone to my own backyard, looked at rare striped lilies.
I have been to police station, courthouse, lawyer's office.
I've visited my husband's body, and tasted it, and consumed it,
    and been strengthened.
    How I dared to marry a good man.
I have been to Nightmare from which Ware is a sweet reprieve.
I've been to the grocery store to buy strawberries and cherries
    and asparagus and almonds and pears.
I have been to Hostile Stare, and seen it soften a bit.
I've been to Ware to visit the Moshers and their cats, dogs, horses,
    home-made bicycles, band cabin where the Cramps play,
    little grandmother's cottage with flowers all around, jeep,
    dump truck, horse trailer, snow plow.
I've taken her to the forests and rivers of Ware, and wished Ware
    were called something else. Somewhere, Anywhere, Beware,
    Take Care of Her, Hairy, Hairless, Harried, Wary, I Take Her
    Out to Warever,
    Wondering if it's Where she should Beware.
    I've visited the possibility of other men and moved away, a mare
    mostly wanting her foals.
Every day I read over how a girl disappeared.
I've visited my backyard, birds squawking, and ratcheting their songs.
I saw a yellow grosbeak dip its beak into surprise July blossoms
on the magnolia. I didn't like the way it forced one new blossom open.

girl turned to stone

The dog's alarmed face

Her feet are terrified, toes frozen apart

The way his hand digs into her thigh

Her young girl breasts partially hidden

How sorry I am for those tender breasts

Look at the grip he puts on her waist

She tries to force his head back

Break it! Break it!

Cerberus can't bear to watch this

The dog has heart

salty

For her, I'd fly into any ruthless port—
And I saw a girl drowned in Cozumel,
I thought she'd fallen to the Great Shark's Court,
I thought she'd sent herself to hell.

I saw a drowned girl in Cozumel,
buying mangoes in the marketplace.
I thought this girl had fallen clear to hell,
till I saw the sweet juice run down her face.

Buying mangoes in the marketplace,
not drowned at all, just hungry.
I saw sweet juice run down her face.
The girl not clutched by sharks, but free.

She wasn't drowned at all, just hungry,
how hungry she was beneath the blue water,
the girl not snatched by devils or sharks, but free.
I want to hold this salty sister.

I thought her fallen to the Great Shark's Court.
For her, I'd fly into any ruthless port.

beauty pageant in sarajevo

The young girls believe
as they parade before my eyes.
They know I have the power
to recognize beauty.

Lana floating, soft as spring leaves
in Sarajevo Park, Biljana's legs scarred
by shrapnel, but slim and curved.
We judges enjoy their willowy forms.

Low-cut silk over delicate breasts.
Where did she get the silk? I ask
and her mother smiles.

*What clothing does a fashionable woman
require? Is virginity important?
What kind of man could you love?*

They hold out their arms like children
selling flowers from the family garden.
They hold out their bodies,

step forward on the runway,
speechless chorus,
slowly raising a large, white banner.
DO NOT LET THEM KILL US.

him

At midnight, his thumbs looked like hammers
even in the midst of bougainvillea and oleander.
My breath moved the petals.
I was afraid of everything.
Throb, throb, went the music, and I hobbled
back barely breathing, lame,
and telling myself his gospel
was not for me.

Irises were my salvation, especially
the purple ones, so slender
and full of rapture.
I thought we would all bloom,
or be broken by him,
but he stroked our throats
as if we were opera singers, longing
for the bandage of his touch.

All hands were waving
in the air, except mine.
I had no love for the holy man,
his draped anger against us.
I am a shoe, I told him,
the better for walking to paradise.
I am a sock, I told him
for keeping my house warm.
I am a peony
in serious opposition.

I need light to sing. Today I drift along,
wings open. How pleasant to be free
of handcuffs and clutter
and all that grease.
After the collision,
I was crippled
by his lips. I refused
to howl and longed for the gaze
of the Buddha, peaceful, peaceful.
Wave your hand, Buddha, unabashed
as you are. Give me gardens.
A bottlebrush tree. I'll no longer
see throats, thumbs pressing
my shoulders, his breath on my face.

return on fireworks night

Careful to be on time, he drives
through fireworks traffic
to pick me up at the bus station.

I'm coming from walking
as far as I could into ocean,
to the furthest sandbar,

from wind that could lift a man,
lift a woman, easy.
Tonight young girls like our girl

parade in short skirts and tank tops.
They flirt with the ice cream man.
The bus driver calls his wife, says

he's running late, meanwhile eyeing
Fat Isabel's curvy rear end,
as the annual boom opens the fireworks

I cannot see, but know by heart.
Soon orange flowers will burst the sky,
and parents lift children to their shoulders,

and stand on the bridge. Be careful!
I want to tell them—the bridge is dark,
and strangers pretend to watch fireworks.

These children should be home in bed,
not out with night parents so different
than day parents all for a few moments

of sprouting red dots lighting up
the broad river, then quiet, and the dark walk
back to the car, clutching those children.

"I've missed you," he says. We hold each other
tenderly, as though one of us might slip away
with a stranger, go off in a burst of light.

iv.
we cannot extinguish the night

"In that city of salt

where my mother walks

with a basket

over one arm—

she's off to market

she's going to buy

all those things

she forgot to give us

when she was alive."

– Gregory Orr

driving toward key west

We were driving in the dark towards Key West,
first in the twilight with marsh and everglades
on our right, seabirds stretching their wings,
water on the right, water on the left. I am not
the lifeguard, and I try not to shiver as we
drive over all these bridges as if there might be one
that took us to the end of the world.
This is not what I wanted to write.
I wanted to write about how exciting it was to head
for the end of America, and Andrew driving
through the night. Bridge after bridge as if
he were driving me through my terrible dreams.
It was a dark night. The sunset burning. The singer
sang about being black and blue.

I am losing myself to several sorrows
though I can get to the ocean whichever way
I walk. I see in the shallows the sand
sharks and jellyfish. I take pleasure
in these living things. I do not know at this
moment that someone I love has entered
the depths. I am still able to take pleasure
in the seagulls and pelicans. I laugh
at the homely pelican, shiver when
I see small fish wriggling in that huge
throat. I admire the pelican's determination
to dive like a blast from the sky down
into the water and come up with small fish
flickering in his throat.

Mambo, Mambo, Hey, Hey, goes the jukebox
from the Paradise Diner. Andrew driving straight
through from Lauderdale to Key West, one key
after another slipping away in darkness,
and our obsessive heading for the last place
on the continent.

It was cold, and he was driving the convertible
with the top down. I knew it was important
that we go into dark over these unknown islands.
At first the marsh on one side, Atlantic
on the other, birds unknown, egrets, long-
necked birds, big-winged birds,

beautiful, and we going so fast over narrow
bridges on and on, closer to Cuba. I feel
like a woman in a dimly lit room longing
for love. Why does the driving
seem so important to Andrew with his rented
convertible, and a wife who's turned into Margarita
under the dark lights of the stars.

Pleasure, I think, pleasure. He wants life
in a convertible, bougainvillea, hibiscus.
We needed this journey, top down, cold,
riding with our coats on through the intense pink,
red finally fading. And the singer "Why do I
have to be so black and blue."

how dare the weatherman

He's a skinny weatherman who gets very excited
about his weather. Cold covers Connecticut
and Massachusetts. Wind-chill 40 below.

States nestle up, two cars bundling
in the same driveway. Cold will drive
these states together if the weatherman

reminds them to stay close, make babies.
He's so skinny out in the cold,
snow coming down on his skinny shoulders, ice

freezing under his skinny feet. He's talking about
the coming snow, past winters, the parking garage
flooded with icy water. His engine won't start.

He'll have to call the tow truck
all because of the weather he delivered.
He's ashamed of his weather.

Inside this room, the table still stands,
no one freezes, but we'll never again
allow the weatherman into our house

to give the report. We didn't know his powers,
don't want to see his bony neck and ridged nose
ever again. We won't succumb to blizzards or ice,

and we certainly won't need Roy's Tow Trucks
to get us moving. Enough hypothermia
to last a lifetime.

sauerkraut supper

What I need now is a sauerkraut supper,
and they're serving it nearby. I want to eat

sour and enjoy it and feast
on it and laugh about the sourness,

and idiocy of anyone who would voluntarily
go to a Sauerkraut Supper, waitresses

in green costumes and pickle-colored shoes.
Why that very person would go on a Swamp

Safari, playing his out-of-tune violin, breathing
rank smells, finding stinkflowers in the moss

and rotting logs. Nymphs emerge from dark waters,
skin glowing with marsh lights. They follow

somberly through the dimness to quicksand.
Not minding the sodden earth, they sink

into the ground, arms lifted to the god
who sends us November, souls full of pain,

and the strength to rise out of quicksand
for a sauerkraut supper where Judas himself
has had a change of heart.

my father blesses the fleet

This bare-chested fellow who doesn't know a bishop from a czar
wants my blessing for his shiny red bike,
and here come all my stout-hearted children
floating by on fishing boats loaded
with cheering grandchildren, all of them waiting
for me to lift my arms.

My daughters married strong men
with arms like fishermen, boats tipping
with heavy loads, waters thick to shore
—swordfish and tuna and salmon and bluefish.
And my son, no weakling any more,
sings as he hauls the lines.

I picture all my afternoons sitting by the sea.
In my old age, they carry me to the water,
hold up my hands, so I can bless them again.
When I'm dead, they lift my red-robed statue,
halo wobbling, mounds of roses at my feet,
bikers and believers standing aside,
each grandchild throwing another rose.

Even now I can't tell myself.
None of them comes to see me.
None of them speaks my name aloud.
I wanted to live my life out in the wind,
but I spent my days   in the ground.

we cannot extinguish the night

I love walking the backbone of the earth,
and lying down with you.

You patiently show me again, Deneb,
Vega, and Altair, the Big Dipper ready

to scoop us up. Night whispers
for us to leap into the dipper and feel

the gust of his breath. We take the stars
for ourselves. Swan in flight, Hercules,

Cassiopeia and Scorpion.
We take these stars, and wear them

around our necks like David.
The well of the sky is holy.

We do not take anything,
but a drink of bright water.

For once we will be content
with the light from our rough bodies,

fires that burn behind our closed eyelids,
desire we cannot extinguish.

bathsheba: i do not want to love you

Does God see us, sitting in darkness,
wrapping our arms around each other,
tasting each other's married lips?

You seem like God
caressing the earth
the way you talk to me in psalms.

You talk to me all night,
love the twilight birds
and rising moon as I do.

I touch the dark hair on your chest,
your soft beard.
You want to take time to love.

You like my long red hair,
wind your hands in it, and pull me close.
You say my hair is a fire on the mountain.

I say God is the fire.
We should be afraid.
You put your hand over my mouth.

the lover

I made him up, the other man.
He was quite a tax collector,
always collecting my lips,
my arms, my gray eyes.
Such a demanding
lover, the draping of my body
with garlands of gardenias
and roses. Our constant tango.
Our constant sorrow. Still
he came by the house
every day, lit the candles,
took out his cello and played
rhapsodically.
So what if he took
everything I had. Locks
of my curly hair, bits of
eyelash, my smile, the gold
earrings my husband gave me,
all my desire, the wrack
of my bones. What woman
would make up such a possessive
lover, one who demanded that I
wear black velvet dresses,
my breasts loose beneath them?
Sometimes I get confused.
Much has happened lately.
The light went out. My husband
is painting our rooms blue.

brazen

I love his brazen legs
in diamond ankle bracelets
holding up the sky,
light flashing from his garments,

his brilliant shield:
the city rises like a bright god.
"Everybody's got something,"
says that little god, the cabbie.

All the people selling glow-
in-the-dark fingernails,
golden hairbows, the Tight Pants
Blues, photographers who

send you down the avenue
to get a kiss from some Cleopatra.
Who are we to this god,
we with nothing to sell,

your arms around me
these many years
soothing my wild eyes
with the garden of your body.

I love your rough beard
and tender mouth, the way
you have long wanted me.
I should be as happy

as the woman who married
the warm earth. If not
for you, I could be one
of those women with orange

hair, six-inch skeletons
dangling from my ears.
I want to stay here,
sing at the Blue Note,

dawdle at the corner
with the bad girls,
be the one with the peacock-
tail fan. If not for you,

I could be the brazen woman
who made love to an indifferent god,
who gave up the whole green
world for love.

the moths

We didn't know whether this was a plague from God,
or were they just little moths? Everywhere in the house,

little fluttering moths. All winter
we watched them, complained about them. In May

we cleaned, scrubbed carpets, threw out
old spices and half-empty boxes of rice and couscous,

piles of papers, love letters I'd written to someone
I shouldn't love. Then everything was revealed, the lies

I told my husband, the musty picture. Little moths
battering their wings. My husband clapped his hands

trying to catch them. Now it was all out in the open.
Our bad housekeeping,

the moths like sad little angels fluttering around us,
and the great, clean house, clean windows, a broken

heart, but open, open,
                        open and clean.

floating back

How to navigate the river of a son named David
at the hot time of day is what we want to know,
and we don't hear the knock.

I dream we are in the bedroom.
We don't know what to do in Africa,
but love each other and walk the beach.

Andrew loves the look of brown women, lets tide
somersault him in undertow, loves the tormenting market,
sniffs pineapples for the sweetest.

Old men thirsty for palm wine shinny up trees.
We laugh at how boys shake down green.
Juice runs down Andrew's face from ripe mangoes.

I like to do the High Life with men whose hips
flow like a river, smoke and dance at Café de la Paix.
Twenty-four, the only woman at my school—

chicken in peanut sauce served over a bed of mpondu—
My students hope I'll dance to James Brown.
I ride on Marvin's motorcycle

and the next day Mutamba asks if I love my husband.
"You don't know these people yet," a Belgian says.
"Do you leave us with joy, Madame?" Mpoyi asks.

Frogs sing near the lake, people offer us all their food.
We fly over the red boiling heart of Nyiragongo,
dive down in our shaky plane with its vomit barrel.

Andrew loses all his clothes—
one yellow shirt
he wears every day, bright canary.

We burn our taste buds—no food ever
as savory. Matuta's sister comes to stay. They sleep
as if at home, gently holding each other.

Andrew says the river is beautiful,
and our child grows in me
as he floats back.

where love is stored

My sustenance,
my daily bread,
my ripe fruit—delicious
as purple grapes,
fresh man warm
from my oven.
I twine myself around him,
thousands of times tighter
than fierce blue morning glories.
He stands over my bed
while babies form
in hurricane season,
afraid they and I
might be blown away
in a storm of blood.
Not something to give away
for the glimpse of a silvery fish,
smooth dive of the humpback,
or the way another man
fills up this room
with his presence.
I tell my husband,
open the refrigerator,
the vegetable drawer,
taste the raspberries in the fruit bowl,
open my satchel, my violin case,
check the packages under the mattress,
love stored in a sock,
a black bra.

men in love with parisiennes

Some handsome friend of mine says French
women vraiment "know how to dress." What do
they do, that we do not? French women steal our men.

Tall men, Small men, Green-eyed men, the Irish and
the Poles. They're migrating to France. Crazy
over French women. Marguerite et Heloise et

Madeline. Ils preferent les femmes francaises qui
faire une promenade dans La Tuilerie—si belle,
si tendre, si douce like the Madonna of the Rocks

in her blue gown. Les femmes francaises make a
certain music as they walk a cote de la Seine.
They eat croissant without dropping a crumb. Sip

a glass of sherry, let it linger on their lips.
They listen to Debussy, light as clouds.
All the men follow longing, longing for a taste

of their French, their French lips, their French hips.
Charmantes, les femmes francaises; elegantes, les femmes
francaises. Soon there will be no more men in Massachusetts

parceque Jean a dit aux ses copains how the French women
with their high heels, delicate ears, hair bien-coiffee—
sont tellement belles! C'est juste que les femmes francaises

ont quelque chose que nous n'avons pas? How to bring
our men back? Nous allons chercher toute la France
pour les hommes! I'm writing from the beauty parlor

as Genevieve lifts my hair off my neck, winds the golden hair into a twist. I've put on my three-inch black leather pumps with open toes. My dress is blue silk. I'm heading

for France to look at those women men love. "Elles sont adorables," disent les hommes. Et nous, nous avons decouvert les Italiens!

taking his name in translation

Margaret Szumowski loves the mouth of her last name,
the zoom that gave her the last name,
the zoom that gave her the oom, the oom pah pah
of a lover, the zooming in of a morning lover, the zoo
of marriage and children, the oom of loving his
delicious self again and again, the ski of the downslope,
and the zoom of the downslope, and the crash on the downslope,
and the strength to ski up the mountain, the bloom of the zoom
of marrying this Polish wonder, Chopin of the West,
the slips and lips of loving him, the ow of some moment,
the awe of his lips, his touch, the groom she always wanted
on skis, prince of skis. The sh of shmovski as it should
be said, the sh of the two of us softly together, the show
of bodies, the moving, the garret of my name, the favorite
garret where I visit the mar that I love so much. What mars me,
and what keeps me, the mar at the edge of the sea. Mar ski,
the love of water, the love of my Polish boy,
the sea of marriage to my Polski, making the mouth
of love to my Polish lover, Szumowski.

the women appear as aurora borealis

One night in the Arctic, we villagers saw the "flashing elements of female souls." The women kept indoors, women whose windows had been painted black, who dressed in head-to-toe black.

They floated out of their houses through the cracks to the Arctic where they could be seen without the burka.

Luminous beauty. Their long black hair, slender bodies from so much weeping, shadows under their eyes like the dark of the moon. *Look, Mother, with your shadowed eyes.*

Soon the aurora of mirth will appear. First their bodies in the sky. Brilliant ice maidens! Then the laughing of the heavens. Then the laughing of the women themselves who prefer the cold, the seals, the walrus, the ice floes, the dangerous polar bear, to the death of the heart. *My mother prefers death to leaving him.*

They are laughing in the cold, and we villagers are making ice candles. See us come out on our dogsleds. Hundreds of ice candles lead the way to the Yypnik village. These women, a gift from the gods. *My father saw her as no gift but his.*

Look how beautiful they are. Northern dancers, we call them. They are not aurora flowers that open and die in a single hour. They become aurora snakes to protect themselves from those men. *Poison him.*

The women are gorgeous feather boas across the night sky. Everything is called aurora in honor of the gods. The aurora of mirth. Hear these women laughing? You have never heard them laugh before.

They fled the harsh husbands who caged them without light.
Mother, you could be all light. It's not too late to seep from the crack he forgot in the east wall.

the room loves her

The room longs for her like a lover, would give her
all its light. The room thinks the woman will be
faithful, here from light's beginning to the last bit
of twilight, taking in every movement of red-tailed hawk
or mockingbird, watching for the first pink of magnolia
or chartreuse haze of willow in the distance. If she
would only stay and dream, the room would fill her
with light. The room thinks the woman does not know
who she is away from its embrace. Spring will begin
with a wince this year, the pain of waking up hope.
Seems as if it would be easier to sleep and sleep under
the earth. The season forces her out blinking like a
creature awakened from under a rock. Huge banks
of snow melt, leaving her heart flooded by the long
winter.

The amaryllis watches the woman with sad eyes. The
woman is a country virgin dressed up as prostitute or geisha
who still casts down her eyes. She is already mourning
the man who will cost her dearly. She is beautiful
in red satin though she would rather be in a quiet house
writing poems and playing her lyre. Liars are
what they are, the ones who sold her.

smart bomb

We were at the priest's house.
My hand shook hard with the teacup.
Perhaps my whole body was shaking.

For days afterward
fat-bellied supply planes
flew low over our backyard

hauling troops to the Middle East.
I was in love with the wrong man.
Outside the earth shook and shattered

as the priest saved the delicate teacup
I had in my hand. I wanted
to shatter nothing,

not teacup, not marriage,
not temple, not Jerusalem,
not one Baghdad café.

Ia in the green spring
(for Michael Carson, 1954-1992)

Lout, dunderhead, tease,
mocker of sisters,
extravagant singer
of too many Falstaffian operas—
we loved him unbearably,
wild man of our hearts
in love with his grand piano,
that kept man, that expensive
lover whom he would touch
in farewell, whenever well he left
the room.

Jesse tends him,
delphinium in the courtyard.
I love to be with him.
Passion Johannes,
Harmonia Mundi,
though when he drops his towel
into the toilet and I pick it up,
I think AIDS, the hell with AIDS,
band aids, pharmaceutical aids, barricades,
knife blades, panty raids, all kinds of Afraids,
but not parades.

Jesse rolls him to the amorous piano.
Michael can touch the keys,
but not play them.

He crumples to breathless,
at the glimpse of green LA.
He's temporary, he's only air,
a fragile kite of himself.
We want him, and he, a pumped-up balloon
in the hospital, sings out, *Hello! Hello everybody!*

anatomy class

They hover around the body
after reading the letter
from the donor.

How much he loved this woman
who bore him three children,
the woman to whom he made love

so often, this body that he loved
and touched even in old age.
Here she is, and soon they will bless

the cranium and open it and look
at her brain and remove it
for further gazing,

and they look into every part
of this woman, not like voyeurs,
but like lovers touching

and naming and exploring every part
of her. She is nothing like the scary red
pictures in the medical books.

She is the body in its beauty.
The medical student says
he loves this body of an old woman,

and he's not afraid to open it and see
what's in the bones. He'll have to crack
the femur, remove the eyeball, what

made it see? What did it miss? Did
she hear everything her husband said
to her? Did her nose smell?

Did the tongue taste? The hands
to wave, to wave goodbye, the nest
of the soul somewhere singing even

as the body is broken down and looked at
and named and poked at until all is gone
and not gone, all gone and not gone.

finally the amaryllis blooms in late february

The freezing snow today is like wafers, the whole outdoors
covered with comunion wafers. I wish I could keep him alive.

Sorrow runs from both sides of my continental divide.
Michael cannot drink water, or eat bread, or sit in the sun

waiting for a lover. Some days evil sticks like static cling.
Whose fault is it? Father wonders. Could anyone have helped his son?

Some people do the wrong thing to survive,
but the amaryllis rose red and trumpeting like Michael rising

from his deathbed wondering when he'll play his next concert.
The amaryllis in its red-robed splendor rises like King of the Opera.

"Dad loves me," Michael says to the pot of earth.
How easy to get stuck when the roads aren't plowed. I have been

dead this night when I hear your voice, Michael,
    see the whole backyard
lit by the hundred year moon.

silhouette of a music stand in an empty room

The music stand is empty,
awaiting music, awaiting a musician.

Shadowy heron
perched on one leg over a twilight marsh,

or the bones of a beautiful woman,
unfinished by the gods.

Who knows what grace
she could bring to the earth,

if they would only finish her.
Silvery skeleton awaits its lyrical flesh,

so much is waiting, bare arms of trees
against a November sky,

those we loved
gone before they were finished,

ghostly herons in a dream lagoon.
I would float out to all these faint ones.

the fence

We have to keep a fence
between ourselves and the hornets.

They sting us once picnic time is here,
and we want to hold each other.

We have to keep a fence
between ourselves and the sky,

can't have the sky push into our house,
and bring the wild birds.

I have twice been the one who released them,
beating their wings against glass.

We have to keep a fence
between ourselves and the stars.

They pour into our brains,
and fill us with searing light.

v.
the unlikely landscape of forgiveness

the unlikely landscape of forgiveness

The way the land itself forgives flood
and grows huge tomatoes the following year,
shoots from black earth, rows of corn shuddering
in the background. Still there is violence in the land,
bolts of lightning that could set the barn on fire,
and terrify the cows. Anger of the farmer
who turns on his wife and daughters.
Thirsty plants, heavy crops,
He studies his little red notebook.
Children and wife too much
for a man under pressure. He could guard them
jealously, as a red-winged blackbird guards his fields,
letting no one near his beauties. He could peck out their eyes.
And the half-blind beauties will forgive him.

no darkness anywhere

Can we say anything new about these old trees
dressing themselves up like young girls
in these flowers, these pale leaves.

I pretend just as they do,
that I am young, that there is no darkness anywhere.
Spring and beauty always win out, I want to say.

Even when there is darkness, the man
beating the pony, beating the children,
aren't there also poplars bending in the wind?

Darkly beautiful walnut trees, lilac thick
in the backyard, noisiness of birds in the Iowa dawn,
and the rich black earth always putting forth

green shoots—the beauty is what remains
and the pain cuts like lightning across
that pastoral landscape.

forget the kiss

Emily wonders if Jesus will hang there till daybreak.
She remembers the cross that swings over the altar.
She thinks this family makes Jesus' ears ache.

Close the door, bring the fire, we need Pentecost.
The priest looks sad as he tastes the wedding cake.
Can these people be pulled from chaos?

If only Michael would play his golden trombone—
the priest feels what untimely death has cost,
yet even in this family, love makes its feeble moan.

Letting the water slap up, was that so smart?
Grandpa loved to ford the river at Devil's Backbone.
How did this family spin out like Earhart?

Emily's afraid Jesus will fall from his flight,
and Grandma forgets to say, "Until death do us part."
What's the good of celebrating—so much spite.

Some refused to come. Preferred a good hiss.
This family frowns, whips up a fight,
won't pretend a marriage full of bliss.

Grandma thinks of Michael, whose death stole her joy.
Grandpa says the vows but forgets the kiss.
Emily wonders how God knows Jesus is his boy.

the knife

Itifewerk kissed my feet on the worst day of my life.
We'd given her a little money. We liked her bright boy.
Ethiopia's beauty cut our hearts with its knife.

The country gave a sudden lurch, trembled with strife.
Her boy sat on our step, whittling a toy,
and Itifewerk kissed my feet, the worst day of my life.

Her beautiful boy. But she was not a wife.
Itifewerk walked to Kolubi, barefoot and holy.
Her faith cut my heart with its slow knife.

Seventy men shot in our street, riven
by soldiers. Nothing to do but destroy.
Itifewerk kissed my feet—the worst day of her life.

We wanted Addis Ababa filled with life
and donkeys and eucalyptus, the usual small boys.
Ethiopia's beauty cut my heart with its bitter knife.

Where were the husbands? The children? Who could be a wife?
Exhausted and feeble, we saw everything destroyed.
Itifewerk kissed my feet on the worst day of our lives.
Addis Ababa, new flower, shredded by sharp knives.

rembrandt's house

Michael has fallen asleep in this bright room.
I wish again I were a painter, as I did in Deerfield

when we looked out over red-gold hills, wide river,
and Anita talked of rare foxes coming to the cottage.

I have seen my daughter in her first communion dress,
house full of lilacs, my husband and children knee-deep

in garden, overcome by all the orange pumpkins.
Now my brother lies in sunlight,

tallest man in the world resting like a baby
in a golden square. Big laugh, outrageous humor—

this is the child who shot a hole in the bathtub
with Grandpa's old gun, lucky that time.

As a young woman, I saw Rembrandt's self-portrait,
dazzled by the light. Michael was caught

by "Christ with Folded Arms" light pouring
from his sleeve.

Same Mozart measure over and over
because he couldn't let it go. His hands at the keyboard,

silhouette of the grand piano in twilight.
An artist with a vanishing subject, I watch.

Rembrandt's house was dark. The light was in his mind.
I want to have the light, paint my brother

laying his long body down on the white couch,
hands resting under his face.

Today, looking at red carnations,
I paint still-life, hold foxfire.

sea wind
(For Michael, 1954-92)

Black feathers and sequins
outside my P-town window.
A huge Drag Queen—
roses, Gina Lollabrigida.
Women hold hands, french-kiss,
men wrap around each other.
Couples parade their town
on a narrow strip
between sea and bay at the end of the earth.
Even Ginny and Kate forget their husbands,
dancing to blues in an all girls' bar—
and the sea wind blows
Away			Away.

Children dive from the wharf
where anything can happen. A boy
carries an infant to watch children
plunge—a great hooray—
unmindful of tourists parading
or boats whose passengers
moan as the bumpy-nosed humpback
opens its mouth.

And I would go out on any sea
for the shadow of Michael's lost body,
find him in the estuary of sleep reborn as whale.
No other body grand enough,
nor songs beautiful enough, to suit this conductor

on a wind-scourged coast pierced
by keening of gull and sough of lost sailors.
This once lost musician
blows his emerald bubble, lunges greedily,
levitates the porpoises and harrows the deep.

I turn my full body to the wind.
I need to know roses bloom at the end.
Michael and Jesse float down Commercial Street,
pink silk suits, roses in lapels,
Forget   Forget

A man-woman is blooming parrots,
and a car floats by: two men or two women
wrapped around each other—just committed,
mad or married,
and I am committed to you, daemon lover,
sea wind blowing through my room
at the edge of the world.

christ goes out in the world

Christ is so large that these muscular young men
can barely hold his dead body between them.

They let him down with bright lengths of Italy,
pink like the houses. They take down his body

and carry him. Mary slumps in sorrow,
on her way to the Vatican with these husky fellows.

In the basilica, she's strong, holds him for centuries.
All the people know how alive he was, how dead he is.

They cry as if it were their sons or daughters.
They'll never recover, but he's off to see St. Peter,

give Mary a break, talk trout fishing or Magdalen's
chestnut hair. He's not so different from other men.

He goes out on the Appian Way to see his Beloved.
People don't notice him walking to the coliseum, worried,

trying to shadow the locals through relentless traffic
for pasta at Carla's Trattoria. He goes anywhere in perfect

anonymity. I notice him in the pensione, offer him bread
and chocolate with his coffee. He says, "I'm not dead,

remember? Invite me for a walk. Match make me
with Magdalen. Give me a kiss. A good one."

night woman's triolet

I fight the darkness from my head
again. I fall in love with light.
But when you take me to your bed

I fight. The darkness from my head
makes you want golden girl instead
of this wild creature from the night.

I fight the darkness from my head.
Again I fall. In love with light.

the old man in the midst of renoir's women

The old man loves the naked women in the museum,
calls to his old wife not to leave him behind
in the room with all the Renoir women,

ripe as apples in his country boyhood.
He calls to her, desperate she will disappear.
She gave him seven children, but one is gone,

and what does it matter now,
if nymphs pull the satyr into the pond,
or if outside, the gardener cultivates

every kind of rose you could imagine.
They are old, their son is gone, but wait,
the old man still loves the old woman.

She is all he has as a woman, rushing away
on bunioned feet. She has spotted the gardener.
What to do about her rosebush

that won't bloom no matter how carefully
she waters, and fertilizes, and waits for it.
She wants this gardener

to be God. "If you had been there,
my rosebush would be blooming.
My young son would not be dead.

Will you revive him?"
"Yes," says the gardener, "He is here.
I woke him yesterday in the palest roses."

bringing the moon to her
for a closer look

The magnolia and its damn blooming caused this ache in me.
The girl knows how to bicycle down Eagle Road and how to
    ride back up!

The deer nibble the daylilies—they eat up all the shoots.
After Cricket's death, the horses went wild. Stalls with their
    bite marks.

With no warning or apparent cause, the window of the van
    shattered.
Now, the girl drives Al's car around the farm. Triumphant
    smile!

I look into the silly, malevolent face of the poppy.
Phony-looking petals, and purplish-black insides, should be
    floating somewhere.

The boats of the dead are floating to Hell.
I think of her as a river.

She is one of those leafy trees again.
Our girl beautiful as metallic bugs, don't you see?

During that time we were all throbbing heart and vulnerable
    inside-outs.
The magnolia tickles me like a persistent pet.

Big crow patrols. Cardinal triumphant in the Japanese maple.
The way he kicked down the door and entered our house
    was a metaphor

for the way he used her. We looked for her in that weird
    neighborhood,
rang the door bells. At every house huge dogs lunged at us.

If only we'd had Snake arrested when he broke into our house.
I don't like men who can make a woman disappear. Mother
    enjoyed cooking

and babies once, but he devoured her. The shadiness was in
    him
and came to be in her. He was a steamroller, pressed on her
    until she was gone.

She taught us to thread a needle, but the needle was too small
for the thread. Every night he pushed into her, but she could
    not refuse him.

She taught us to make may baskets, and drop them on boys'
    doorsteps.
She taught us to be may baskets dropped on boys' doorsteps.

When Lyle called, I was afraid. "You'll never get a date that
    way," Mother said.
Each morning I sit by the magnolia, take on its endurance, its
    ability

to flower when no one expects it. Black-eyed susans survive
    drought
and downpour. Today my girl is lighthearted enough to sing.

I wish I could bring the moon to her for a closer look, but my
    soul is too shallow
to hold all this beauty. Looking for nectar after my night of bad
    dreams.

eve's list of what keeps her from despair

The way hummingbirds hang in the air beating their wings and sipping the nectar

Fireweed rushing in after forest fire to hold the earth in place for seedlings

Adam working in the garden, admiring his lilies, his blue globes, his butterfly bush

Turtles congregating on a rock. More turtles congregating on another rock

A snapping turtle swimming in the reservoir, sees me and dives deep, as if shy

Walking every day to North Truro to run on the sandbars and feel the wind

Babies in my arms, at my breasts, on my lap, cooing, crawling, wobbling, gobbling

Walking round the reservoir, sweet lake smell, turtles, grumpy geese, purple loosestrife

Forsythia, lilacs in every backyard, peonies fragrant, poppies, delphinium, daffodil

Shiny skyscrapers, fat ballerinas, sailboats on the Charles, cormorants directing traffic

High heels, black nylons, slim if it could happen again, BB King, Brubeck. Baby

Just Look at Me Now, Writing the Blues, Listening to Blues or Jazz or Flamenco Guitar

Tall men, smart men, funny men, kissable men, ticklish men, pushover men, theatrical men, Poetic men, musical men, more men, grocery store men, hospital men, circus men

animal-loving men, baby-loving men, outdoors-loving men, movie-loving men, etc. men

Rhapsodies, Goldberg variations, Rachmaninov—she knows how to spell it

This is the beginning of what keeps her from despair

columbus avenue on the night of the lunar eclipse

In New York City we are standing on the sidewalks
of Columbus Avenue looking at the moon disappear.
We are dressed up and silly in high-heeled shoes.

We should have a lunar eclipse party!
We see the shape of the moon and for once its roundness
like an unknown planet seen in a movie.

At last we know the moon—
no shimmering eye that could blink out
and leave us alone, but solid

like a man with a strong body.
We forget this darkness
wait again for the full moon that crazes us with desire,

bring out fire batons, tap shoes to celebrate.
The moon is so round,
we could take it in our arms.

bare-handed

Once the father watched a striped snake
catch a struggling toad. The hinged mouth
stretched wide. The snake undulated
from the yard, the toad in its mouth.
Today the father does not slump like a dead man
in his chair. He walks along the river
enjoying yellow butterflies, deep
frog voices, the rush of water,
water so clear he sees the bottom stones.
Today, he surprises his wife. They'll tube
the fast river. He hasn't thought
of tubing or canoeing for years. He's been old,
imagined his daughter dead Ophelia floating.
That goddamn guy.

This year the father's garden holds Siberian
irises, orange cat-faced poppies, bleeding
heart, miles of daisies breezy
under the apple trees. So simple sic ling weeds
in the flower bed. "Not like trying to get rid
of other things around here," he thinks.
He's a man who likes a wild flowerbed
full of black-eyed susans, bold lilies, sky-gazers.
How to tear the fear from his mind?
Still the growing of delphinium and cosmos
makes him lift his arms to the sky.
When he turns, there's his daughter lifting
a cigarette. One other thing he can't stop.

He could kill that guy bare-handed.
As he walks by the river, he knows
he and his wife will lie down under their
dark starry sky. They'll see Deneb, Vega,
Altair, Swan in Flight. He'll finally
put up the purple hammock.
Even his girl is out on the river.
It's hard for the father to believe,
his girl, pale, wading the fast-moving river
on a scorching day.

how far I would go for you: to the distant trees

For his disobedience, I drape him in vines. He fades into
   bunches of trees.
Blessed as I was, I offered prayers to Allah tied to bunches
   of trees.

Wasn't it fun, the day I draped him in peonies, and he
   fell into my bed?
Everybody laughed at him, frizzy hair, drunk among trees.

Your shoes and socks, unmatching. Your clothes punched
   with holes.
A wedding tonight. I'll see you two lovers bunched naked
   under trees.

Stop it. It's wrong of you to speak always of grief. What
   about hope?
Thousands of antelope crunch ripe fruit under persimmon
   trees.

A girl blessed. A lyrical child for so long, not marble, but flesh.
She climbed the birch with its dangling arms, munched
   apples in trees.

The country we loved is not a bower. It's a desolate place.
If Shahid returned to Provincetown we'd bless him, lunch
   under trees.

I've paid in fingers for losing you. Put a sock over my face,
   throw me under the bridge.
I'm not dead, but disobedient. The tyrant love crunched my
   heart under the trees.

Margaret is at a certain age, we must bear with her. She shimmies under trees.

Let's get her drinking wine, rapping and tapping, punch-drunk under trees.

acknowledgments

"No Darkness Anywhere," appeared in *The Christian Century*.

"Beggars' Opera" appeared in *The Massachusetts Review*.

"The Old Man in the Midst of Renoir's Women," appeared in *Spoon River Poetry Review*.

"Silhouette of a Music Stand in a Empty Room," appeared in *Calliope*.

"The Knife" and "La Fiorentina," appeared in *Crab Orchard Review*.

"By the Light of Her Flaming Baton," "Night of the Lunar Eclipse," and "Beauty Pageant in Sarajevo" appeared on *Tattoo Highway* (tattoohighway.org).

"His Fingertips" and "La Bruja" appeared in *Three Candles*.

"Taking His Name in Translation" appeared in *Blue Moon Review*.

"Him," and "Tough Customer," appeared in *Diner*.

"She is a Nation," and "Self-Portrait in a Helicopter," appeared in *Poetry Repairs*.

"Salty" appeared in *Hollins Critic*.

"At the End of Their Driveway" appeared in *Barrow Street*.

"We Cannot Extinguish the Night," appeared in *Chrysalis*.

"Smart Bomb" appeared in *Another Chicago Magazine*.

"Eve's List of What Keeps Her From Despair" appeared in *Poetry Midwest*.

"Woman Trapped in a Tree," appeared in *Americas Review*.

"The Woman Who Gave Up a Good Thing," is now "Brazen" and it appeared in *Willow Spring*.

"My Father Blesses the Fleet," "Black Swans in an Iowa Springtime" and "The Heron Flies Fast Over the River" (currently titled "Bare-Handed") appeared in *Segue*.

"Rembrandt's House," "Taking His Name in Translation," "Anatomy Class," "Huge in His Great Robe," "The Moths," "Christ Goes Out in the World," and "Asking for the Bread," appeared on *TheScreamOnLine* (thescreamonline.org).

"Night Woman's Triolet," first appeared in *Ruby's Café*, a chapbook of Margaret Szumowski's poems, published by Devil's Millhopper Press.

"Floating Back," appeared on *Szrine* (szirine.com).

"Translation by Water," will appear in *Tattoo Highway* (tattoohighway.org).